MW01177845

A Spiritual Journey

shedding the light of the
Lord through poetry

TATE PUBLISHING & *Enterprises*

A Spiritual Journey

shedding the light of the
Lord through poetry

written by
Megan Elizabeth

photography by
Pamela J. Butler

TATE PUBLISHING & *Enterprises*

Published by Tate Publishing & Enterprises, LLC
127 E. Trade Center Terrace | Mustang, Oklahoma 73064 USA
1.888.361.9473 | www.tatepublishing.com

Tate Publishing is committed to excellence in the publishing industry. The company reflects the philosophy established by the founders, based on Psalms 68:11,
"The Lord gave the word and great was the company of those who published it."

Book design copyright © 2007 by Tate Publishing, LLC. All rights reserved.
Cover design by Janae Glass
Interior design by Steven Jeffrey

Published in the United States of America

ISBN: 978-1-60247-507-6
1. Christian Poetry   2. Inspirational
07.07.19

Dedication

To God, for without Him I would have no life to live, no
future to see, no words to write, and to my Grandma Ruby,
may God bless her abundantly.

Contents

The Hearing of Faith

Do you ever have memories that replay over and over again? They're like a movie with a crisp and clear picture. The sounds are muffled a little, but I can still make out most of the noises I heard. A big memory just came back to me again. I don't know what triggered it, but it came like a blow to my gut. God said many years ago when I was twelve, "Go home, say bye to your mother, stay up an hour later, and I'll wake you at 4:30 a.m. with a surprise. I wish it didn't have to come to this, but I want you in My arms! I want you to return to me! You are a key to bringing My children back to Me, and I must change your life now by whatever means! Your cousin will be okay. I have something in store for her, too, but I will take him home with Me, pain free. By My hands you will get through this, then you will be Mine. No questions asked." After that, I felt wrong about spending the night at my friend's house, especially since my mom was leaving at midnight to go camping, so I went home. Step One completed.

I stayed up until she left, said bye and I love you, then went to my room. I can't remember what I did during the hour I waited, but I finally went to bed around one o'clock a.m. Steps Two and Three completed. Then came His will—all working out as smoothly as I am writing this. I was facing the wall, and while I was sleeping, my name was being whispered, "Megan, it's time. This is the time I take you back. Wake up, Megan." Without feeling the tap on my shoulder, I turned over. Hearing the voice, I opened my eyes. My plan was to go back to sleep, but my plan was not the one that won. Red and yellow lights began to dance in front of my eyes. I took a double take but continued to see the same thing. My breathing became more rapid. As I hurried to the end of my bed, I looked out the window and saw fire trucks, two ambulances, and police cars surrounded a crumpled up station wagon that had crashed into a tree. Step Four completed.

My mind was blank. Nothing was going through my head—none of the usual dreaming or analyzing or anything. The devil and all his lies couldn't even reach me. I ran downstairs and found my dad, brother, and his friend by the front door, watching. It was my cousin's car. She and her boyfriend were in it. *She'll be all right, but I will take him home.* He went instantly, *with no pain,* but she remained trapped in the car for an hour. I watched the whole thing from the sidewalk in my front yard. Step Five completed.

If she had only stayed awake for a few more seconds, it would have never happened. Wait a minute! There was no way out of it. She was going to fall asleep no matter what. God's plan always comes through.

The Holy Spirit tells me to look back at the morning of August 21, 1996. Those few hours changed the rest of my life. It took a few years until I was fully in His grasp. A few more years passed until I realized the truth. Through everything I had been looking for was the Holy Spirit. The Lord says to me, "Do you want to know how much I love you? Look at what I did when you didn't even know My love. Look at what I did for you!"

Thank you, Father, for finding me. I wouldn't want to be anywhere else. I dwell in Your kingdom now and forevermore.

"Now may the God of hope fill you with all joy and peace in believing, that you may abound in hope by the power of the Holy Spirit."

Romans 15:13 (NKJV)

LIVING IN DARKNESS

Unaware of what lies all around me.
Living in darkness is where the journey begins—in darkness
before the sun emerges ...

The Journey

I feel weightless
Gliding over the land
Through the clouds
Up, up, up
Higher, higher, higher
Where am I going?
Out of the atmosphere
To the infinite stars
I keep going
Into the brightness
With more fluffy clouds
And blurriness

Eternal Life

Send the best out
Not the prettiest
To the earth to
Help the lonely souls
As they remember the birth
Of a new lifestyle
Tell them to be brave
As they are flying to
Their only real freedom
Do not be afraid
To fly into
Eternal life

Shadows of the Past

People come and go
Through life, it never stops
Smiling, laughing, crying
If only the going was natural
We'd all be better and happier
Coming is great fun
Being loved and cared for
Loving and caring for someone
The going has to be so hard
Don't ask why, it just is
Some cringe at the moment
Some cause the moment
The black ruthless hearts
They are the ones that should cringe
Not the innocent, the guilty
Ruining a child's life
Saddening a loving spouse
Scarring family near and far
Bruising the heart and soul forever
Living the rest of eternity with the shadows of the past

I Was There

I was there while you were sleeping
I was there to stop your weeping
I was there to be your friend until the very end
I was there to let you know
That you were free to go
I was there when you said, "No"
I was there to change your mind
And help you find your reasons why
I was there to fly by your side
Which no one else could do
I was there to guide you through
Because I was there to be your Angel

The Way Things Are

I understand other people's opinions
I understand how a mother loves her children
I understand why people want to
be important in their lives
I understand the meaning of life
I don't understand all the violence in the world today
I don't understand why someone
has to waste his or her breath
I don't understand why people have to rush
I don't understand why people hate
I think I will listen to the world
I hear the cry of little babies with no mother
I hear the cry for help
I hear the sound of gunfire
I hear the wolves howling
I hear the sound of beating hearts
I stood in a meadow and looked at all
the colors of the world
I see every race as one
I see reflections in the water
I see red and black hearts
I see other's pain as my own
I see my future
I stood in the city and smelled the car fumes
I smelled the horrible stench of blood
I smell the fear of people when they don't need to be afraid

I smell perfume as other people pass
I smell the seasons come and go
I feel safe almost everywhere
I feel the pain of victims
I feel my mother's warmth
I feel happiness
I feel the kindness at Christmastime
I think about the future breaking down
I want people to be happy
I want the future to be a safe place for my kids
I want the hunger to stop
I want random acts of senseless kindness

Blue Over the Horizon

... Looking above at the dark blue sky
I see glimmering stars and a pale cheese moon
Over towards the horizon it turns to a brighter blue ...

Finding Forever

Look beyond your heart and soul
Can you find it?
That warm, fuzzy feeling telling you everything is the way
it was planned
That feeling you get when you look into your lover's eyes
and see your souls holding hands in God's kingdom
Remember seeing your mother smile like an angel, and you
swore there were wings peeking out
See that long-lasting reunion with your family and friends
It feels like Christmas all over again,
but this time it's here to stay
The laughter of a passing Angel with the appearance of a
child you once knew
Do you feel the power of knowing that you're in the right
place because of who you are and what you did?
Well, then you found it

Steps to Eternity

The brilliant colors first led the way
Every kind of flower ascended with it
The purples, yellows, pinks
Green vines wrapping themselves around the goldenness
The ancient steps kept going into eternity
They spiraled through the clouds
And into the stars
Past the planets and moon
The purples, yellows, pinks
Green vines wrapping themselves around the goldenness
Each step brings you closer
A smile springs upon your face
Then stop …
You look up …
The magnificent gold is almost blinding
The gates open as you take your last step
Weightless clouds surround you
When you are inside …
You look around at all the faces
And know that you are home

The Pain of Love

Love hurts, there's no doubt about it
How else would you know what it is
The only pain that your soul feels is love
You can love someone so much that it hurts
It's a feeling that is an endless explosion
Releasing brilliant flames of fire that set you ablaze
You become confused and wonder
why you feel pain within
It never leaves, but some choose to ignore it
They can't handle the pressure their love penetrates
Only the strong can go on but everyone does love
They just might not feel it because all the drugs and abuse
stand in the way
But it breaks free from the dark corners within
I feel it growing inside of me, I can't help it
I'm addicted to the pain of love
I would never get rid of the pain it takes to love you
Always and forever will I burn for you

Dying

What will it be like when you die?
First, you're all alive and can see things through your own
eyes, then you can't …
Are you scared before it happens?
Do you panic? Do you smile? Is it okay if I'm afraid to die?
I don't like pain. Will my death hurt?
When will it happen?
How did the people on the plane feel right before they
crashed on September 11?
What was it like to get a phone call from your daughter who
was just calling to say goodbye, because she
knew she was going to die
I wonder if anyone on those planes were ready to die
They had no choice
Because of that people might lose their faith in God
They can't understand why God
would take them so violently
But their names get to be engraved
on a huge stone wall by the rebuilt buildings
Maybe I would ask God, if I were given the chance, "How
do you decide when and who to take and how?"
That would help answer all my questions
I know it's His will and that's what needs to be

The Growing Heart

My heart is growing
It must be what the feeling is, it couldn't be anything else
I get quotes to help me understand
There's nothing wrong with that
Don't do things alone, but I'm not
I have the best offense a spirit could wish for
It'll help win this fight within
My heart is growing and my soul feels it
All this love is going to be released in an
explosion of heated passion
I will smile and it pours out
My spirit is ahead of the game
She's on her turf
She makes the rules
Tame the being
Work together
Stop tearing me apart
I won't let go, I will not let you have your way
I want the pain, not the fight
I want the burning pain to continue
It's the only way I know I'm alive
The burning pain of love controls me
My heart has spoken
The being is almost tamed
With God's help she will be completely under my control
I will live with the burning only to love forever

My heart has spoken
My soul has generated it
You can't stop the burning

Thinking of You

I just thought you would like to know
That I've been thinking of you
Thinking of who you are
Thinking of how much I love you being a part of my life
Thinking about your soul and all the
wonderful things consumed by it
Thinking about your heart and hope
it's kept safe in the hands of God
Thinking of how you can make me happy
by just one simple smile
Thinking of how you are so sincere in honest love
Thinking about you is something I will always do
Your heart is safe
Your soul is pure
Your love is golden
You're in my thoughts where ever wherever I may go
You're in my thoughts, forever

Constant Battle

There is a constant battle between
good and best inside of me
The burning is so strong and powerful,
I know it must be true
Who will win? Who do I want to win?
The being or the spirit?
The being breaks rules
She's selfish right down to the core
No boundaries will consume her
She wants something and she'll fight to the end
The spirit feels right, though
All time, happiness, and peace
Seeing things the being does not
Showing me things nothing else can show me
It'll never let me go
This feeling is consuming me, controlling me
I'm the audience watching, in horror,
all the fighting and fire
Who will win?
The one who fights past forever
The one I want
My heart, my soul
My spirit

I Will Remember

I will remember
The way your laughter glowed like an angel
The way we talked about nothing at all
The way you smiled and looked in my eyes
The way things used to be
I will remember
The good times and the bad times
Every worry and every doubt
All the sunshine and the laughter
All the thunderstorms and tears
I will remember
All the gatherings
Every glowing face
Every whisper, every spoken word
Even if it wasn't meant for me
I will remember
When I have no memory at all
Your touch
The sparkle in your eye
The love in your heart
And even the times I don't want to remember
I will remember
The hurts, the worries, the wait
The glory, the truth, the freedom
The shadows of our past will help us remember all
I will remember you and you will remember me
Because I am a part of you and you, a part of me

Imagination

Imagination
My thoughts
Anything I want
God gave everyone
Including me the gift of imagination
Nothing can stop it
Always in my mind and heart
Today and everyday for the rest of my life
It never leaves me alone, I won't let it
Oblivious when it strikes me
Night and day my imagination rotates around me

Angel's Playground

I want to be on a cloud!
Up with the blue sky and cotton soft, pure white cloud
Too bad it's the only true white,
everything else is dirty and worn
Nothing could be whiter than the clouds in the sky
I want to fly!
I want to take flying lessons so I can at least fly through
those clouds, if I can't lie on one
I want piano lessons! I'll feel like I'm on that cloud
The weightless feeling the keys project raises me higher
into the pure sky-blue sky
The sight and feeling of being so high would be
exhilarating
The sound of the whistling wind swimming through my
ears with a hawk's cry …
And the heavenly sound of piano talent
The smell of freshness as the infinite sky surrounds me
I'm higher than the birds, they can't touch me
Mine! It's all mine! This freedom to sit comfortably playing
the ivory piano keys
A hawk lands on the cloud piano she stretches
out her wings
I don't move as the hawk's eyes mesmerize me
I begin to play a song I never knew
The song of heaven, the song of peace and eternity
I like staying where the angels play

GREEN FOLLOWS AFTER

… Rolling to a lime green as the trees create a ziggity line …

No Regrets

It's just me and my thoughts
What He has left me with is what I ponder
My future lies in front of me
My career plans have also begun to curve on the road
My hope is growing into new things
Fear and worry need to be thrown in the trash
I lock Satan in his own closet
This time he will not control me
Nothing can be a backseat driver to God
There's no such thing when He's behind the wheel
I am going to do His will for Him, not for me
I could turn my back just this time
But if I did, I would be giving in to the devil
I would be turning my back on my Heavenly Father
I'd have regrets
I have to be the sponge and soak up the chances
I'm realizing now what He is doing
He tells me to do this
He wants me to read my poetry, His words, out loud to
people who aren't blood family
I feel it'd be wrong if I didn't
This has gone farther then I thought
I pray that He will bless me, knowing He will
I pray that He will spread His word through me, knowing
He will
I pray asking, knowing He will answer

A Gift

Poetry is my gift from God
A gift to live
A gift to give
A gift of thought
A gift from God
A gift from the most prestigious being
A gift to let go and be free
My gift is kept in a safe
Inside me is where my gift has made a home
A gift to live by
A gift from my God
I love my gift
I love my God

The Father

It's so great! Crazy great!
The glory
The joy
The peacefulness
I believe I'm in His grace
Everything is better now that I've found Him
And it was right in front of me!
The wind doesn't blow the same furious way anymore
The sun doesn't cast angry rays
The rain doesn't drop to drown or flood
The sun doesn't set in magical clouds from the spectrum
He paints a painting in the dawn and dusk hours
He pours water from white barrels to feed His creations
He turns the heat on to warm the cold,
skinned flesh and ground
He breathes breath for all to live
Why? Why does He do this?
The Father's love of His child is heartfelt
It's joy!
It's glorious!
It's the sun setting in brilliant pinks and purples!
It's the way the rain creates a bow of magnificent colors!
It's the yellow ball of fire keeping us from turning blue!
It's the whistling wind!
He is telling us He is here … there … everywhere!
Not just in the eyes of His children, but in the body of His
creation

Your Will Is the Road I Will Follow

Shine Your light where my road leads
Bend the forks and pave the ground
Open my heart to the people passing by
Show me through the darkened tunnel
Empty out my mind and send in peace
Guide me over the quick-sanded trail
that may lie in front of me
Help me to understand everything and all
Shine Your light where my road leads
Bend the forks and pave the ground
Open my heart to all creations
Show me the way to my future
Light the candles and blow out the torches

Signature Flash

The flash of lightning possesses an emotion from God
Who is He angry at, if He's angry at all?
The lightning doesn't come from heat
or coldness like the weathermen say
It doesn't come from a mixture of hot
and freezing or whatever they may think
It's a signature from God
Signing His piece of art
With one magical bolt the task is done

The True Christmas Feeling

It's not about gifts or money
It's not about whose tree looks the prettiest
It isn't any competition
Or some publicity festival
It's something new and different
It's something special and powerful
It's a part that has been hidden for too long
It's a warm feeling in your gut that belongs in your heart
It's something that I can't forget
It's something that I can't get enough of
I hope it will happen again and again
I know it will because it's inside of me
It's not just for Christmas
It's not just for me
It's for families everywhere, everyday
I understand now
The emptiness I thought I felt has been filled
The honest and true Christmas feeling has prevailed
No more gifts or money or competition
Just You

Inspire Me

I'm on a roll!
Wow! Everything is flowing through me!
Feels like it'll never stop, I love it!
I don't want it to stop
It's like a medicine,
it's a drug giving me power to keep going
My blood is boiling, but I am left cold
My heart sings, but my mind is thinking too loud
Keep it coming, don't ever stop!
I beg and pray to You, God, don't let it stop!
It's not bad, it's actually good
I'm not being selfish, am I?
I don't want to be selfish, or jealous, or unloving
Let me love everyone and everything
I say right here, right now, please don't ever take it away
If it is taken away, then who am I?
My belief in You would not exist
I want to believe in You, and since I do, I can do this
You are my medicine, you are my drug, my ecstasy, my
hopes, my dreams
You are embedded in every corner of my heart
I need You to live!
I need Your soul in mine!
You have to be there
Never leave me, never let me go
My inspiration is You, and I can feel You inside me

Thank You! Thank You for You!
Thank You for love to give!
Thank You for my mother's love! Thank You for You!
I pray to be able to do this forever!
From my heart to my hand, please let me be powerful!
Amen!

Whisper to Me

When will He send me more?
When will my blood simmer?
When will He lock the windows of doubts and negativity?
I know the truth of the world
I know logic has nothing to do with it
I know You are all the truth I need
I know what You are going to do to me
I know it may be soon
I know it may take awhile
I feel it there inside me
Tell me what I have to do to release it
Send me signs to help me make my decisions
Tell me what to do
Tell me what these thoughts mean in the written world
Tell me what You want to say
Write it down, whisper it to my heart
I know the vacancy is not permanent
I know my whispering heart will never cease
You are my whispering heart
You are the water that makes the river flow
You are the air that makes the wind blow
You are the sun growing in the flowers
You are the raging thunder behind the stormy clouds
You are the pouring rain from the blanketed sky
When I walk, I walk in Your handiwork
I will always walk with Your presence inside me

Tell me what needs to be said
Don't let the whispers linger any longer
Send me what I need to do and let my memory tell me
when I wake

Carry Me

My heart beats on this wakening day
Oh, what a glorious day it is
My breath flows like a peaceful upstream river
My eyes wander over God's creation as I brace myself upon
entering the windy air
Questions are always unanswered,
thoughts always untamed
There are reasons never found,
never understood, some never sought
My mind is only made when allowed
Carry me on Your back
Over the land and through the clouds
Around my eyes and pass the stars
Carry me to eternity
Answer my questions there, show me the reasons,
and feed my thoughts
Carry me on Your golden wings to where
life begins and forever rests

Kingdom Come

God's kingdom will be inside everyone
There will be a time when I will know Him the way He is
His greatness will be shown to my eyes
His kingdom will surround me everywhere
The pure desire will stay!
My heart will become pure
My soul living on through eternity
I will be there when this day comes
I will fall to my knees when overcome by His glory
I will be there to touch His face, to be pure
We are not able to understand the purest
heart until we reach eternity
The second coming of Christ is upon me, it is upon us
Reach salvation while you can
God's glory will shine it's brightest
Peacefulness will overpower me
The sky will open
Into the sun-shining clouds will He descend
He will take me away
He will take the faithful home
There will be that day when history does change
I will be there in one form or another
His whisper in my heart becomes
louder as I follow His path
Once I reach eternity, I will know Him
My heart will be as His

Send me to the needy
The ones who need You
Send me to show them who You are!
Send me into Your will
Let the whispers become shouts!
Send me to have victory over the enemy!
You will lead me to eternity in Your kingdom
All my life, I had not known the pleasure
I have not had peace of mind
I was in the grasp of evil
Plaguing my thoughts, my ways
My life had not been His, it was mine, so it seemed
He was prepared for that
He was prepared for everyone like me, and not like me
He knows when the second coming will be
I had not known grace
Salvation meant nothing to me
It came though
Somehow, some way, and maybe someday I will know how,
but now I know why
Love is the greatest reason
Love of life through eternity
His love for His children is why
Before my time, He had seen me
He knew I would need salvation
He knew I would need love
He knew my sins would be forgiven by Him
He knew I needed His love
He knew me when Jesus died for my sins

He knows me more than I know myself
I know why, I will learn why
I will learn how, I don't know when, but I know why
His love, my pure desire
His love, my faith
His love is my salvation
Eternity is a gift that comes with salvation
His love is my grace
I'm in love with Him and only Him
My true friend, my true love
His kingdom has been seen by my eyes
His love is here to stay inside me
I know there're other things He has, but love is what it
comes from
My life is His, I know that now!
I am not afraid
Plagued by evil is not possible
I am a child of God
You are a child of God
We are children of God
Let the Father be proud
My heart whispers secrets when I sleep,
even when I'm wide awake
Secrets of the night, secrets of the day
Secrets only I will know, but be heard by everyone
Secrets like these are meant to be shared

Yellow Breaks Through

… The green melts to a lemonade yellow
It's coming brighter than ever …

Given Signs

The other day I was watching the sunset
I was on the road going home, and I was
staring at the western horizon
Throughout the day, God had been sending
me pictures in the clouds
Just above the horizon where the sun would
be was a jagged line across the sky
To me, it looked like it could be a far-off hill or mountain
A few minutes went by and the sky-wide mountain cloud
began to point up in one area
It looked like a temple or something along that line
I chuckled a little, and said, "The kingdom of heaven."
I thought that was great in itself and my imagination was
going overboard today,
Then another few minutes went by
A pinkish-yellow cloud formed at the
top of the mountain cloud
I saw a being with His arms wide
open and slightly leaning back
I was drawn to it until it hid from me again
He is waiting in His kingdom for me,
for you with His arms wide open

Jesus

Jesus, my Lord
Jesus, my rock
Jesus, my salvation
Jesus, my Savior
Jesus, my love
Jesus, my everything

Desire In My Heart

My desire swarms all around me
I feel the heated passion in invisible smoke around me
Then I wonder if my desire is real
Or am I just trying to be like the others?
Never would I want to be anyone else
My desire is honestly true
I look around at my surroundings
He created that, and this, oh and these too
Nowhere I could go to get away
I don't want to get away
Lord, please, don't let me slip away
Grasp Your hands around my wrists before I fall
Catch me before the jagged rocks break my body in half
My desire, hold on, I can see Him more clearly
I just open my eyes and I can see His shadow in the light
I only have to stare out my window to stare into His eyes
I listen to the birds and I can hear Him singing
I press my face against the window and look at His world
His world is for His children, it's so magnificent
With a gentle breath the clouds roll across the sky and
everything else sways in the smooth current
With a flick of a finger to a switch He pours the rain down
to splash into puddles
I jump into the shallow water just to feel it on my flesh
The beads of love drip down my leg, replacing itself into
the water

My desire is to take all this in, to feel it always
My desire is to dance around the moon and stars
Play tag with a comet flying through time
My desire is to die and to live in truth
My desire is to see and smell the
wonders of God's universe
My desire is to taste God's honeysuckle tears on my lips
My desire is to hear the cry of an eagle,
thanking my Father
My desire is to touch the heart of the universe
Lord, let my desire burn

Your Gentle Touch

When You touch me …
My nerves tingle throughout my body
But it starts in my gut
Proceeds like the ripples in water
That's just the beginning of what You do to me
Reverberating in my soul
Electrifying me with Your presence
O, how I feel You deep inside me Lord
I cannot ignore
Your power surrounds me and swallows me into Your
creation

Binding Faith

I believe in the unknown
I believe in the unseen
I believe in knowing what stands behind the curtain of life
I believe in the spoken truth and the unrealized fact
I believe in everyone who puts forth the effort to succeed
I believe that life is a gift, and at death, you receive eternity
I believe that God gives me these gifts and gives me the
choice to act on them
I believe Jesus died for everyone!
I believe God's angels are sitting right
beside me as I write this
I believe there are no walls in any reality
The lines continue to be drawn through space and into
tomorrow
I believe this is not me who writes
It is not a muse, or a leprechaun,
or a figment of my imagination
I believe that God Himself is the writer, which I can't fight
I believe luck is only a metaphor, used by the devil to drive
the faithful beings away from God
I believe coincidence is just another word for God's will
I believe people need to be shown the ways of the Lord so
they can believe
I believe in everything I have written
Through my heart the Lord speaks to me
Through my tasted tears He heals me

Through each smile and word He spreads
I believe He can't be stopped
For I believe everything is hidden from the naked eye

Tomorrow

With a kiss of light
The morning breaks over the horizon
The day begins with a touch of the Hand
Rapid people hurry off in their routine
Stay out of my hair, Satan
I long for the touch that brings light
I run off track
Desperately searching for You
Seeking Your warm smile
Touch my skin
Hold me close
Everything is fine …
With You surrounding me
A mountain of hope waits for me
A river of life flows for me to drink from
Depression is Satan twisting my life
Blocking the light with a fist of sadness
The Truth is stronger than the brick wall
When it bursts into slivers of shame
The light shines, surrounding me and through me
He is all around, caressing my life
I look at Him
Stare into His promising eyes
Everything is fine
Tomorrow is new

The future awaits His will
Tomorrow there is new hope
Tomorrow is a day closer
Tomorrow is You

Gentle Flower

Gentle flower standing on the shoreline
Don't be afraid to stand amongst the pebbles
You reign amongst them
All the others have faded but the
shoreline is where you remain
Oh, gentle flower, spread
Let the breathing wind carry you to another destination
Gentle flower, float towards me, grow around me
Sprout a new world
Entrap me in your vines bedded by the buds
Spread around my neighborhood
and only prick lurking evil
Change the appearance of the crumbling world
Gentle flower, spread beyond my feet into the salty waters
Spread beyond the towering mountains and fallen cities
Tangle your vines around my trembling heart
Spread, gentle flower, spread
The caressing feeling needs to be known by my neighbors
Gentle flower, do not hesitate,
but rapidly change my world
Gentle flower, along the shoreline
I smell the presence of heaven

Swept Away

Set me free
Make wings from my back
Lift me as a feather
Guide me away
Deeper into Your soul
Falling into eternity
Heart pumping heavier for You
Life clinched in Your hands
Roaring flow of blood passing over
Serenity in the river's flow
Peace dancing around my body
Joy tickling my senses
You stroking my hair
Paradise in Your child's eyes
Heaven awaits my presence
Falling ever so lovely for You
Smiles spring from my lips
Eye contact is made
The love in them swallows me whole
Everlasting in Your presence
You have swept me away

The Greatest Sacrifice

I know this song
It says to me …
It was not a mistake
It is not regretted
It's not anything He would change
It was for me
For the children
I hear somewhere
"He saw each and every one of our
faces when He was crucified"
To me that means …
Instead of seeing His life flash before His eyes
He saw my life flash before His eyes
He saw every soul flash before His beautiful eyes
Not just the children in His time
The children in all time
From the day He sacrificed
To the day He comes again
It is the greatest sacrifice of all
Above all
The sacrifice of the Holy Human Lamb
His life for my sins
What else could I ask for?

Secret Riches of Life

Let me write all the letters of my heart
All these emotions and love for You
Let them pour out of my soul
Exclaim them until the river runs dry
All my heart can hold
Let them be known
I want to know my heart's secret
Don't keep it to Yourself
Let me in on all You know
Secret riches of life
Unbury the treasure
Secret truth in all the land
I want to explore all the secrets
Let me in on all Truth
I will share with all I know
Your truth and Your secrets
The hidden riches I will seek
Placed where all can find
If they seek with the right guide
Secret riches of my life
Hidden with gentle care
Hidden with love, grace, and power
Hidden in my heart

Precious

Your breath in my lungs
It's precious
Your love in my heart
It's precious
The rising and setting of a new day's sun
The voice of all the morning birds
They're precious
The growing of a spring flower
Smell the essence of the Father
Small buds growing into a green leaf
They're precious
Laughter of my family
The laughter of God's children
Send that gleeful smile my way
You're precious
Your sweet, sweet love
The light I see in your eyes
You're precious
The mercy and grace I receive
It's precious
Everything You have done for me
It's precious
The gifts I have and will receive …
I will always hold close to my heart
The love of family and friends …
Will always have a place inside my spirit

The love of the Lord ...
Stands strong with me against all trying to harm me
Father in heaven, You are precious

I See Him

I see Him through the clouds
Winking at me from the stars
I taste Him through the raindrops
Trickling onto me with pure softness
I hear Him through the singing birds
Roaring waterfall dances rhythms all around
I touch Him through the hearts of His children
Running fingers through the hair of His creations
I smell Him through the essence of each flower
Pansies to roses, dandelions to vines, everywhere
His touch is in everything around me
The fullness of Him sits on my back, guides me through
His presence kisses my cheek in the morning sun
I smell Him through the freshly fallen snow
Each glittering their praise to the Creator
I touch Him through the scars in my heart
All the things from the past tearing me all sorts of ways
I hear Him through the rushing of ocean waves
Leaves blow in the whispering wind,
sing to the sky, song of heaven
I taste Him through the freshly grown apple
The sun brushes against all He creates
I see Him through the smiling eyes of my mother
Love seen by the blind
I see Him in me

Your Eyes

Your eyes full of laughter
Laughter shared with a friend
Your eyes full of tears
Tears from a heart of many years
Your eyes full of love
Love that can run the world
Sent to me as a mother
Meant for so much more
God gives everyone special gifts
I have everything I need
I have everything I want
The softest kiss from the morning sun
The gentle hum from the singing bird
The purest touch from the crisp blue sky
Sweetest taste in the driving rain
I have everything I want
I dwell in the house of love
I have a gift from God
A gift to write
So I write to you
Because without you I would not know God
You are more than a mother
More than a friend
Treasures are shared between you and me
You've guided me into the path for God
I could say more

But it all comes down to this
You are my angel
And into your eyes
I am mesmerized
All the laughter I see dancing in there
All the tears fighting for God
I see all the love in God's great world
Through your eyes

The King

I stand amongst others in the battle of life
Our swords are ready to fight for what we believe
Standing strong, we are ready to die for our King
The soldier's heart is never dying
No fear for knowledge of what may come
There is no earthly king who would fight for his people
The soldiers who die may never see their king
The truth
There is a heavenly King
The heavenly Father
He put Himself aside
He died not for Himself
The King died for His people
Every person in His great love
The King gave up His life to save His kingdom
That's what the world needs
That's what the world received
A King who died for His kingdom
The King turned the rules of time
He didn't wait for His people to take the fall for Him
He stepped up
The King became the Soldier

He's Everywhere

He's in the wind blowing my hair, whispering
He's the sun warming my skin, healing
He's in the rain wetting the earth, caring
He's the thunder echoing the air, being the Father He is
He's in the hawk's cry, way up in the air, watching
He's in the chirping birds cheerful talk, teaching
He casts the clouds across the sky, behold the beauty
He's the man on the moon crying for the sake of His children
He's the stars in the sky, lighting the way
He's the light at the other end
He's the ground I walk on for support
He's the air all around, giving me breath
He's the night, He's the day
He's in the light, He's in the dark
He's what I lean on when I walk
He is the Father of the universe
All things He does are for Him to be known as that Father
He's waiting at the end of the tunnel

Life, Love, God

Love, laughter, all things worth living for
Imagination to explore the unknown,
to expand on the truth
Fruit to all Your children in all the lands,
they hunger for You
Everlasting harmony, peace, joy, love
Lifting me higher, light my path with Your love
Only way to live is through Your grace
Vile enemies will not take me away from Your love
Everyday I see the love more and more
Glory be to You always and forever
Obvious to my eyes is Your
hand gently holding the universe
Death never lives around Your love for me

ORANGE CONSUMES THE SKY

... The sherbet orange pushes the previous colors to swallow more of the horizon ...

I Am a Poet

A poem is a song the heart sings
That's where it all comes from, the heart of my soul, at the
place where the warm, funny feelings live. I know it's there,
because it gives off energy and burns
Scientists use their minds, but poets use their hearts
The mind is a place for smart people
They make discoveries and cure incurable diseases and
travel to the moon and back
The mind is for the lawyers and doctors who save your life,
except they didn't save mine
Something more powerful than the mind, something that
scientists can't prove and never will, has saved my life
My heart belongs to that undiscoverable being
A spirit that has given me a second chance to see things
His way
I now see things differently and with more color
I want to share what was given to me with the world
The powerful feelings that swim through me are written
onto paper and the pressure that sat on my heart is gone
But it comes back and feeds me more
I feel relieved and strong
My beliefs are free and can be shared with the world
What kind of person would I be to keep it all to myself?
I don't know how to save a life, I might be able to, but it's
not in my control
I'm not a scientist, I'm a poet

It's You

I was completely touched by You, Lord Jesus,
when that song came on
It felt like I felt Your pain and despair
Jesus, You are my passion
Never will I lose You, Lord, my King forever
My passion will be shared by the world
They will feel You inside them
The way the sun warms their shivering skin
Your love will warm hearts day and night
They won't know what hit them
We are here to show them it's You
It's You who makes the time tick by
You who turns the earth around in orbits
The stars twinkle from the touch of
life You placed on them
You make the birds sing and the cows moo
You make life in Your chosen children,
Lord Jesus, it is You
You have chosen to bring life into this molded shape
Your hand has shaped my life
Your love has captured my heart
Let me release Your pain to others in an explosion of fire

Set Me Free

I sit on a bubble wondering when it will pop
I bounce on it trying to hurry it along
It remains fully bubbled, not giving way to anything
I have no clue if this bubble is good or bad
When will I know?
The shadows lurk around me in mysterious ways
My eyes dart around the room to catch them in action
Unsuccessful every time, left wondering
what the movement I saw was
Receiving no clues, or am I blind to the obvious?
Do I have to learn something?
Do I have to figure it out myself?
If it's right in front of me, it's invisible
It's all a part of the growing process
To experience this will reach me closer to maturity
Seek Your guidance, You tell me ... all right
Lord, I pray You guide me to the
things You want me to find
Show me where to go
Help me understand
Lord, I want to be Yours
You have taken me in a gentle jerk into reality from a world
going under
Never let me fall back into deterioration
Let me not slip into oblivion
Be my rock against my tumbling back

I will not fall when You are standing strong for me
Words cannot express how thankful I am
I become speechless when wanting to tell You how much
my heart yearns for You
Touch me now and send me soaring into Your glory
Spread mercy upon me and let me touch Your face
Your soft skin brings pleasure to my fingertips
The desire spreads to my hand and sinks deeper to my arm
Spasming in a rejoice to You
Your beautiful face calms my quivering lips
The sweetness of your cheek leaves a
twittering buzz on my yearning lips
The touch of Your hand on my chin
sends me in a delightful trance
Do not pull away, for I am lost with the
pleasure You allow me
Thank You for being a pleasant master
I willingly accept my duties as Your
child to spread Your truth
Your secret will be known to others I know
Truth is all around me
Spread like the wings of eagles and soar into the lives of
Your needy children

My Reason

No one else comes close to the love You give to me
When I didn't even turn to You, You have loved me
You were thinking of me,
even when I wasn't thinking of You
I can see the love
I see the blood
My sin is red all over Your Son
Thank You, Jesus
Father, thank You for this Lamb
"It is finished"[1]
Now I've found the choice to be free
I am free
Reign all over the land
You will storm Your way through each life
They will worship You as I worship You
No one comes close to Your almighty power
Power to give victory over the enemy
All power belongs to You
All love is Yours
Once, it seemed You loved me for no reason
I've found it, the reason
I wake to see Your glory
I close my eyes to see Your face
I breathe to show how You work in me
I talk to give You praise
I sleep to wake in Your new day

I love and feel love for a reason
I live for a reason
No one comes close to You
My reason

Truth

God is the top
He is the bottom
He is always in between
Remember, if you hit rock bottom …
God is your ladder
Your strength to get out
Remember, it's not you who reaches the top
God gives you mercy and grace to get there
Don't make Him bring you down
If you don't recognize His hand in your life
You will be knocked to the floor
God is your ladder
You will crawl before Him
There's a way around that
Start fresh
Love Him in the beginning
Glorify His name in everything
He is my everything
Let Him be your everything
Without Him, life would not exist
Without his love, I would be doomed for eternity
He has loved me since the beginning
He loves me now
He loves me until the end
He will lift me to the top
Not you, not myself, but only Him

He will bring me home
I don't like being lied to
God is the truth

The Good News

Don't you get it?
Why would you not choose something so great?
How would you feel?
To give up your child for the sake of others
Would you want your child remembered in vain?
Wouldn't you want people to
appreciate and love the sacrifice?
Especially if it was for them
For those who sinned
For those who did wrong
How would you feel if those people took for granted the
death of your beloved child?
If they thought nothing of it
I know I wouldn't like it
If I gave up my child for the lives of the world
I'd want them to be grateful
But since I didn't, I can appreciate
what has been done for me
Do you get it yet?
Why our Lord and Savior gave up Jesus Christ, His Son?
For us who sin
For us who get plagued by Satan's evil games
I recognize the sacrifice that came for us many years ago
This world is not controlled by demons and fire
That ended long ago, it won't come again
No more doing wrong with evil play

No more saying, "Should," and then turning the other way
Your sacrifice has been absorbed
Spread the blood, oh Lord ... Spread the blood
And as for you believers and nonbelievers ...
Understand what they mean, on that day when they placed
Him on the cross
Recognize that He died
For you

The Soldier

When a soldier dies in a battle for their country …
How do we treat them?
Do you remember them giving their lives in a sacrifice?
Do you bless their family?
Do you thank the Lord for their brave soul?
I know men and women, young and old, who died
They died for this country's freedom
Jesus was an army of His own
He stood for what He believed in
He obeyed the commands of His Father
Isn't that what soldiers do?
They fight according to what their commander says
Jesus went willingly
He sacrificed His home, His way of life
He gave His life
Jesus is a true soldier
The ideal soldier
Never complained
He was always honest
He fought and died for our freedom
Not freedom of human rights, like what Americans fight for
But freedom of life in eternity
Without His sacrifice, we'd be living in a crumbling, boiling,
forsaken, driven by demons, volcanic world
I won't imagine the "what ifs"
Jesus is the true soldier

Crumbling Walls

My wandering mind rolls along this bumpy road
The ground is shaking on these trembling thoughts
My capacity of thoughts won't be
able to hold this bumpy drive
What will it be like?
The walls are starting to crack and rot in the corners
Will the clouds look so different and even more beautiful
than I usually see them?
Will time have stopped?
The white paint begins to chip as the
cracks spread over the four walls
Will there be a blinding light ... but pain free?
Will the wind blow and gently caress my tired skin?
Will the sounds of the world
die in this magnificent minute?
The crackling becomes louder and my ears start ringing
Will animals know it too?
Will my kitty know who it is and not run and hide?
Will everyone in the world know what's going on?
People of all kinds, will they stop and watch it happen?
Chunks are beginning to pound on the hardwood floor
The ceiling is coming down and the walls are folding
What will it be like for all creations on this coming day?
I believe we will know it
Even if you are an unbeliever ... you will know
Will it be an instant flash of lightning

Or will it take some time?
I don't want to be trapped in this caving room
The power of God's promise can
crumble an entire city into dust
The secret of the truth can bring upon you a wave contain-
ing all water in every ocean
The power of the truth will set you free
Leaving no room for my wandering mind
The walls have crumbled and
all that is left is a pile of stone
I wonder no more
Now … I wait

The Provider

You are the provider
Nothing comes close to Your power
I am a seeker
Nothing I would rather do than to seek Your wisdom
Seek the glory You give
Seek the wisdom You share
Seek the love of Your heart
Seek the blood of Your Son
I seek for the truth in Your eyes
Provide the way
Provide the means
Provide the wisdom
Provide me the way to shine Your love
Provide me understanding
Provide me strength to stand in the midst of my enemy and
to have victory over them
I know what Your love feels like
I know what Your Son has done
I know my heart, my soul, my life are all in Your hands
I know the wisdom You tell me is from You
I know the Provider provides my necessities and my breath
My provider whispers secrets inside my heart
My Lord and Savior, You are the Provider

Long, Long Ago

Long, long ago my sins rested to death on a cross
Long, long ago my sins no longer held me captive
Long, long ago was too many years before I was born
Before all things I know came a Man
Who died for me
Who didn't know me but knows me most
Logic is frightened by this
Runs and hides in the bushes
Long, long ago there was a Man
Covered in blood was He
My sin lay all over Him
I was known … long, long ago
I was given a chance … long, long ago
Long, long ago, there was a Man
A Man sent by God, the Father of the universe
This Man, I am proud to say, is my Savior
My idol is this Man
I want to be like this Man
To die for my Father's glory is what I've done, will do
This Man died for me
There's nothing logic can prove
Reason is love
Nothing too hard to explain
My God loves me so much
He's given me my world
He gave me His Son

There's nothing to it
I love His beloved Son, I will have everlasting life
With my Father, the Son, the Spirit
The sacrifice for me, for the world
"It is finished"[2]

Passion

I wrote it and then I read it in a book
Then I cried at the way He did it
Maybe my passion is to tell people that He died!
Died for you, for me, for us all, and that's the good news
That is why I didn't read it first
He wanted to show me in His awesome way
How He is my words
How He can show me what He wants
Lord, is this my passion?
My whole body was boiling
Heat from Your touch penetrated throughout
Wow! The Holy Touch can goose up my flesh
It sticks my hairs straight up
Lord, You are inside me
A raging fire in my heart, below my heart, my soul
Your love has stuck to my bones
Dear Lord, You are electrifying
Holy is Your touch, Your strength I feel
The powerful boulder is rolling along my muscles
Dear God, You're magnificent in Your Holy gown
A heart-pounding pulse is not dying down
O Holy Spirit, Your golden hair is blinding me
Melt my skin, O Holy Being
Shine through my blood
Let it pump down the stream of eternity
O Holy Ghost, You are here!

You're shivering my skin, Your warmth is all around
You *are* God
And I am Your messenger
The world will know
I have found my passion

He's So Much More

Jehovah
Immanuel
Carved in stone
Almighty
Lord
Loved forevermore
Father
Holy Spirit
Surrounding me
The Potter
The Painter
Beautiful works of art
The Creator
Great I Am
Master of the universe
The Planter
Life giver
Omniscient One
Gentle Flower
Rising Sun
Glory be to Him
Son of God
Son of man
Trinity is complete
The Lifesaver
Soul Keeper

Born in the womb
Sin Redeemer
Lamb of God
My Everything
Salvation to all
All the names He possesses may run longer than the sky
One name explains it all …
Jesus Christ

Giving Up

I've given it up
For all the world to see
What was not mine
The trials and tribulations
Heartbreak and despair
Guilt and death
Giving it up
Life that is not mine
Death that does not belong to me
Giving it up
Sin is no more
Death is dead
I've given up looking for another answer
There is no other answer
No more searching for the lie
I've given up despair
All my sins have been given up
Everything I am
I am giving up my life
To freely live in You
Since you gave up another life
For me, You gave up Your Son
I'm giving up my life
To belong to You

The Crown

Amber glow
The golden radiance
Stare into those eyes
Beautiful eyes
Eyes of compassion
Eyes of understanding
Eyes of love
Eyes of sorrow
Spray His blood
Fall to your knees
The golden eyes of my Lord
The difference of inhuman eyes
Yet born of man
The will of God, not the will of man
Feet bare
Stomp on temptation to save Himself
Whipped and beaten for the children
The familiar words of the gospels
Tears fall in the embrace
Paradise is just beyond the horizon
Oh, Jesus my Lord
My salvation was not easy
Heartbreak and red, red blood
"Father, forgive them, for they do not know what they do"[3]
The truth is nothing short of my desire
Passion burns in the spirit within

The explosion is never ending
My soul is secure in the river of blood
"For God so loved the world that
He gave His only begotten Son,
That whoever believes in Him should
Not perish but have everlasting life."[4]
The crucifixion, so be it

You Are

Hear my heart cry out for You
My deepest desire flares
From the secret place in my heart
The passion burns in my spirit
Your presence is the fire inside
I love You so much, You have melted Your way in my soul
How could words possibly describe it
I'm thankful You don't need words
Feel the fire You have given me
Thank You, Jesus, for Your scars
Jesus, You Are
You are heaven's shining light
You are the universe's twinkling star
You are the colors of the world
You are the sounds of the earth
Jesus, You are All
You are the blood flowing through my heart
You are the river of tears streaming down my face
You are the fire inside me burning so fierce
You are the air flowing in and out of my life
You are the words in all my world
Jesus, You are worthy
You are worthy of my sputtering
You are worthy of it all
From the scars of Your body
Jesus, You are worthy

The Father in heaven gives no words to describe it
Everything You have done for me …
I am more than thankful
Because You gave Your life for me
I want my life to be Yours
All for what You Are

RED BLEEDS BEYOND

*… Each color is a shade darker, but none darker than the next
The cherry red is last to be seen before the blinding orange ball
consumes my vision
The sunrise rainbow, only lighter than the sunset, has come
and has gone until tomorrow*

Your Name

I will shout Your name to the soaring eagles
Carve Your name in the rocks of the mountains
Send Your name in a bottle across all the waters
I will sing Your name to the resting birds
I will write Your name in the dirt with a heart around it
Your name is permanently written
everywhere on this earth
Stitched in my heart is Your glorious name
Jesus Christ, my Lord and Savior
My salvation, my love, my life
I am devoted to You, I will never go
I will never be lost when You hold my lantern
I always worship You, my Lord, my Master
Father, all Your creations lay in front of me
They will not be ignored, I will cherish them as my own
You have the power to do as You please
But You brought me, gave me breath
Giving me a choice, a chance to follow Your way
To achieve salvation through Jesus Christ
You knocked on my heart
It finally opened, jam the door to keep it from closing
Your name is stamped on my skin
Your name is known throughout the world
Your name is praised from country to country
The animals all around know Your name
I know Your name and what comes with it

Your name brings love to my life
Because of Your love I have salvation
I will be like You, Jesus, my Savior
See You tonight, tomorrow, through eternity
In Your name

Because Of You

This is my final resting spot
Always surrounded by Your brilliant colors
My life is more than what it used to be
Because of You my life means so much more
Because of You my life is important
Because I matter to You
Because I give You all the glory
Because I couldn't live without Your breath in me
Because You created me too long ago
You are the Creator, the Father of this universe
You are Truth
You are the Meaning of life

All Mighty

The man asks the towering tree,
"Do you know who planted you?"
The leaves whisper inside the breeze,
"An Almighty Gardener."
The same man walks along side the beach and peers down.
"Who placed you under the sea and along the shoreline?"
The grain of sand responds,
"The Almighty Truth, and I travel far."
The man wanders into the forest and gazes at a snarling
black bear. "Who gives you the right
to growl your stained-teeth sharpies at me?"
The bear becomes silent and gazes through the clouds.
"An Almighty King of the jungle."
The man crouches by a flowing stream of spring water.
"Who allows you to cascade over the rocks?"
The rapids dance along the pebbles.
"The Almighty River of Life has broken
me off and let me run free, here, so I may spread."
The man peers into the snowy-white mountain tops.
"Who let you grow so high?"
The mountain shouts in a soft whisper,
"The Almighty Hand."
The man hears a rumble of thunder and asks,
"Who gave you permission to speak?"
The rumbling clouds respond, "The Almighty Voice."

The man goes to the sea and stands along the surf. "Who allows you to roll along the sand and far beyond?"

A roaring wave responds, "The Almighty."

He goes to a singing bird
sitting beside a nest of chirping chicks.
"Who is the creator that placed breath
in you and a song in your heart?"

The chicks answered, "Don't you know who your creator is? Who breathed life into your lungs and placed love in your heart. Dear man, do not fret, for our creator is your creator, the Almighty God."

I Am Coming

That's what I came here for
You're what I'm coming for
Just like I've done before
It is I who you adore
That's what I've come here for
Be certain I will come for sure
To save those who adore
It is you I come here for
To show you I love you more
Turn to Me and you will see
Everything you were searching for
My heart will make you pure for sure
That's why I will come again
To bring home your family and friends
To show you my love never ends
It is the world I come here for
How I will cry to see some go
But you will rejoice in My arms
Your brothers will rejoice in My presence
You are what I come here for
To give you peace and love in eternity
You will touch My face and I will hold you
Your smile will ever glow
I am coming for you

Save Me

I am being plagued by thoughts not from You
Help me block them out
Be my strength in all light and darkest hours
Be my rock to lean against, O Heavenly Father
Slam shut the open window that allows the doubting
thoughts to swarm around my head
O Lord Jesus, save me from making the wrong decisions
I love the way You hold me when they come
Block them from my eyes, Jesus,
lead me to the right decisions
Lord, You are my rock and my strength
You are the stepping stone on which I climb

My Everything

I love You, Lord Jesus, and all Your holiness
The glory of my Father is all I need
Your heavenly name is all I worship
Lord Jesus, You are my everything
I wouldn't dream of having anything else
My everything is all I'll ever need
In Your chosen time, I will soar into heavenly gates
In Your time my life will be Your glory
I'm not my own, but truly Yours always
I love Your glory being all around me
Jesus, wrap Your arms around my skin
Make me Yours
Make it known to the world that I am only Yours
I love You, Lord Jesus
My Savior, my Father
My Rock, my Strength
My thoughts revolve around You, Lord
You are the center of my universe
My Jesus Christ, I am Yours
Never will I turn away from the
safety I feel from Your touch
I don't want anything more than to be Yours
You are my Everything and always will be
Through life and eternity I will worship You only
I will worship my Everything, forever

The First Prayer

A man praying for the first time
To stop the enemy from grasping him
He prays hard as the enemy hands reach
His soul is true
Fingers stretch closer
His heart is taking the full lunge
He is believing for the first time
His heart is honest
He wants the enemy to leave him
He wants his sanctuary
To be home in eternity
His first prayer is the stepping stone to a better life
The wind blows
The enemy has left

Living for You

My heart is Yours, O Lord
My heart is Yours
Take it and do as You please
O Holy Being, take my heart
Make it pure like Yours
Take my life, O Holy Jesus
Take my life in the palm of Your hand
Change my life, Heavenly Father
Change me to be as You are
O Gentle Holy Man, change me in Your image
O Faithful Father, I am Yours
Yours to fulfill Your will
Yours to show Your glory
Yours to spread Your gentle wave of love
Yours who You created
O Lord, I will live for You

Leap of Faith

I am wading in the river of God's love and righteousness
The soft current against my feet is gently moving upstream
into the unknown waterfalls that
cascade down ahead of me
On my back I carry my Father's love and His word
Every step is a step closer to the beginning
Swarming around my head are the
doubts and worry of failure
The hopelessness attempts to bite at my skin
I swat them all away with a hand of faith
and spray them with God's promise
The troubled sky is cleared away by the
only truth I was searching for
The shining rays of His smile warm my blue skin
I take a bigger step in the steadily flowing water
The sand beneath my feet will hold me forevermore
I do not sink, I do not get stuck, I do not slip on the slippery
cover the sand turns into mud
I do not stagger, for the stick I walk with is
topped with an angel of guidance
My journey is growing fierce
The thunder talks in the distance,
I am still here, Just keep going.
I am not afraid, for He is with me
The worries with wings will not cause
me to utter in the chill of the water

They give me a reason to grow in my
faith that my Father is holding my hand
I creep to the edge, peering down into the foaming mouth
at the bottom of the water cliff
The only way out is to take the leap of faith
I can't get through this by going back or to the left or right
I must only go forward to follow the path of my Father
All is still around me
The bugs that swarmed around my
heart have fled from the thunderous noise
The wind is the breath of God whispering in my ear,
Do not stop now. I am still here.
I remember the thunderous sound is His voice
My arms spread
I make the leap

I Have Been Found

It does remind me of my immortality
It's nothing I need to be afraid of
I don't think I am, God knows how I feel
If I really am fearing it, He will know what to do
Dear Jesus, my Lord and Savior
I praise Your Holy Name, kneel over,
and kiss Your gentle feet
Help me through, Almighty God
Help bring my unknown secrets to the surface of my mind
I want to give them to You, but I don't know what they are
I'm sad for a lost soul, who may never be found
I fear the enemy has taken him behind locked doors
Will he remain there through eternity?
Thank You, Father, for keeping me
I know You won't give my soul to the enemy
Thank You, Holy Ghost,
for protecting my soul, keeping me safe
I will always worship Your holy glory
I'm sad for the lost soul,
who may never be seen by my eyes again
But at the same time
I'm grateful I will never be lost
I'm grateful for Your holy blessings in my life
Thank You for never giving up on me
Jesus, my Lord and Savior,
You gave up Your life for my salvation

Now I give You my life
Because of You
I have been found

Thanksgiving

I'm thankful for the sun
It warms my skin in the cool October breeze
I'm thankful for the blue sky and blanketing clouds
A passageway into heaven's eternity
I'm thankful for the green grass covering the dirt
A soft spot to sleep under the twinkling stars
I'm thankful for the dirt at which we were molded
Into a body of Your image You created me
I'm thankful for the flowers and trees
Bringing heavenly smells to my senses
I'm thankful for the singing birds
Waking me every morning with a warm kiss to my cheek
I'm thankful for the turning of time
That brings me closer to the steps of eternity
I'm thankful for the sparkling
water all over this green earth
Water brings life to all it touches
The falling rain bleeds into the ground,
promoting it to be stronger
I'm thankful for the gentle breeze stroking my hair
When it blows, the presence of You is near
I'm thankful for the day, everyday,
which brings me closer to You
Everyday is new with new possibilities, new opportunities
I'm thankful for the night,
a chance for You to place Your hands in my soul

My dreams are visions from You
Bottom line is … I'm thankful for the universe
An endless line of Your glory and Your power
I'm amazed by what You have and can do
You can create anything You choose
But with that … You chose me!
You wanted me
So with a breath of air, I was born
With a single touch, I know love
Your love brought me to life
You clipped a string of hair from Your head
You placed it on mine
You touched my bones and gave me skin
All I am is a glory to You
This creation is Your ideal for me
I am not my own
Never was and never will be
Your strong and powerful hand
did not just create the universe
You created a unique creature in resemblance of You
You created the creatures of the world
I'm thankful for the effort You gave in creating me
I'm thankful You want me the way You created me
I'm thankful for my life
I'm thankful for the opportunity to live it
I'm thankful for Your mercy
Your glory will be known
I'm thankful for that whispering stream,
the river of life flows through me

My word is Yours, and I'm thankful for Your will inside me
But the most important thing
I'm thankful for Your sacrifice
Now I have the chance to be forgiven
My sins can be erased only because of Your Son
I'm forever thankful

Forgiveness

The world is unfair
Treating anyone and everyone with injustice
Working for the evil enemy
Only to corrupt the lives of the children
Strangling every innocent soul
With the reins of their sin
Leaving no room to breathe in a dark and dreary world
World of the flesh, hear my Savior
He is not of this world
He speaks in the rumbling storm
He burns for you in the fire of your heart
World of the flesh, there is only one Hope for you
Seek it and you will survive
Love it and you will not be
sucked into the path of your sin
What can the world's unfairness do
If you possess the power of your soul
Do not stand in fear against the forthcoming light
Reach out to it and be saved
By the gloriousness of the One
So what if the world drags you into the ground
Go to your knees and pray
against the enemy hacking at your soul
Go in victory over the flesh and its selfish ways
From my Father this comes to you in all the truth
Feel the fire in the forgiveness of the Lord

The darkness will fade in the paradise He offers
Ask for love and forgiveness
He *will*, without any doubt, find His way to your heart

I Choose You

I'm not sad
For I know where I'm going
I know what needs to be done
I'm not sad
I'm glad it wasn't me and I rejoice
The love within me gives me the right
Who knows where you go
At least I know where I'm going
I didn't sit on the sideline and ignore
So I'm not sad
A lost soul won't be found again
But it wasn't me
My soul is found
The choice was made
So has mine been made
Two separate choices
If that's what really happens
I'm glad it wasn't me
I can't be sad for someone who makes their own choices
I did what I could in prayer and love
The choice is theirs
I made my choice and it will never change
I love you, Jesus
I choose You

There's Something About You

There's just something about the way You work
It's something amazingly, fantastically beautiful
There's just something about the way You work
The gentle hush of the rolling waves
The sweet kiss in the morning breeze
There's just something about You that grabs hold of me
The way the sun caresses my skin
The sky covers me wherever I go
The trees whisper Your name in the fury gusts
The birds sing their praises as they fly in Your glory
There's just something about the way You love
The stars twinkle in the darkest night
The moon casts a white light over my road
The universe is endless for my roaming
This earth is a gift to Your creations
There's just something about Your power
The night and day will always come
Tomorrow is all that matters
The past is yesterday, behind me forever
There's just something about Your glorious name
That I only want to shout it across the land
The mountains will rumble in the sound of Your name
There's just something about that
mysterious way in which You work
That nothing can compare to
The thought of something better crumbles into dust

Blows away in Your breath
There's just something about You being in my life
The reason why I'll have everlasting love and happiness
The reason why I go on in Your will
There's just something about You,
I have finally figured it out
The love in all the world …
Cannot compare to the love You have for me

My Love

My love is deeper than the deepest ocean
My love stretches beyond the sky
My love surpasses every built road
My love reaches higher than the tallest mountain
My love for you is hotter than the blazing rays of the sun
The sky is no longer the limit
Each cloud is a fluffy pillow to lay your head on
Each flower shares My essence
My love is the air you breathe
My love is greater than any other
My love lasts longer than life
You are surrounded by My love
Each day caresses you in a powerful embrace
My love never ends
My love came down
I wanted you
My love came down
My love gave you another chance
My love forgets the past
Dwells in the now
My love fights for you, not against you
My love was reborn
My love came down
My love is everything you need
My love reigns
I have and will always love you

I'm Here

I've begged …
Let Me into your hearts
I don't want you lost
I've pleaded …
Come back to live for Me
All your heart's desires will be met
I've convicted …
Judgment I will have
Give Me a reason to bring you home
I've sent My Son from My side …
To make you free from all things evil
To keep you safe from sin
To block your soul from eternity below
My Son died for My children
I have given you all
You have given Me nothing
I'm here
But are you
Come to Me to know My love
Seek Me
You shall find Me
Love Me
I'll always love you, never ending
Love Me
You'll see loving eternity
My Son, My beloved Son …

Died for you
Just you
Die in Him
Live for Him

He Can

Every heart that breaks
He can mend
Every soul that is lost
He can find
Every life that is doomed
He can save
Every path filled in darkness
He can light
Every pain in every body
He can heal
Every sin in time
He can forgive
Every hole dug by the enemy
He can fill with life, love, eternity
He can do all things we need
Oh, He can heal the broken body of a desperate man
He can heal the sorrows of a childless mother
He can
Because … He has
He can hold you up when no strength is in you
He can rest your mind to sleep when stress keeps you
He can never let go
He can show you paradise
Can you
Can you kill the old and let the new come
Can you die in yourself and be reborn in Him
If you can … He will

More Everyday

Shout to the Lord
Shout of praise
Shout of victory
Shout of worship
Always worshipping You
On my knees
On my face
Singing praises forever
Your word is Your promise
How could I not declare Your beautiful glory?
Shout over the sea
Carry over the echoing mountain
Your name will be heard by people
They will fall in Your presence and worship forever
I'm so in love with You
No one comes close to You, my Everything
My desire soars beyond the stars
Passion dives deeper than the sea
The old me died and I was reborn
Held in Your arms I reached the surface
Gasping for air You breathed in me, love me
I'm so in love with You
Never will I deny You
I need to know You, Lord
Dreams are coming alive
I found my true love

More like You found me
My heart is open
I am in love with You more everyday

Gracious Forever

My heart flutters in thought of You
My lips smile in realization of You
My soul dances in light of You
My mind sings praises of You
Each day the same joyous way comes from You
My mornings become brighter
You hold me so tight, the warmth devours me
Sensation of freedom and glorious love
Consume me with all of You
Overcome my thoughts and let me be glad
My future filled with hope in You
Dear Jesus, my truest Friend
My Savior, I love You the most
Brave Son of God, You sacrificed for me
No language could explain my thanks
My action will help
Let Your will swallow me whole
Your truth reigns in me
Surround me in Your love
Forgiven from the cross, I am free
My sins washed away in blood
Gracious forever, Lord Jesus
My passion burns, my Salvation
I am in for good, happy forever
Delighted to be safe in Your arms
My future is secure in Your will

I guess what I am trying to say is something You already
know
Thank You for the view, my revelation was so clear
I am so thankful, I can only show You and give praise
Worship You I will always do
Through my life I am Yours to fulfill Your will
Through life and eternity I am forever grateful

Soaked In Love

What drives me is the clenching inside
Tighter and tighter as the song goes on
I can feel Your love inside me
My soul jumping against the walls of my body
My soul wants to be free
To hold You tight and return the love for good
I know the love is all around
So what makes those moments so different
The feeling penetrates me
Reverberating along every nerve until each feels the power
Explosions inside me burst out in tears
I feel how much Your love is
Too powerful for the mind
Enough to release my soul and let it be free
Take me away in Your love
Drift me to where we meet
My insides quiver as the song comes to an end
The tears fall to the bottom of my chin
I love You so much, Lord
Taste my tears and know how much I love You
They drench my face for You to know
I feel what You have done for me
Inside and out, it's all for You
You melt me into a puddle
I am soaked in love for You
I can't explain it anymore than a song
But You know and continue to love me more

Resting Spot

Sometimes, I want to stop
Stop fighting
I just want to lie down all day
No more fighting
Some days, I can't stand the fight anymore
I feel weak
Unable to go farther
Unable to stand
I lie in bed and cry
My cheeks become soaked in my tears
My eyes drown in sorrow
Loneliness creeps around me
My mind drifts deeper into the night
My tears subside as I rest my head
On Your lap I lay my fragile body
Running through my hair Your hand dries my tears
The child in my heart rests in Your arms
My eyes close as the sound of You calms me
You are my resting spot
My start and my end
Whenever I feel down
To You is where I will turn
I can cry in Your arms without shame
I can recapture hope while in Your lap
My strength comes back
I can fight again

With a deep breath I walk forth
Knowing You will be there again
Tomorrow it will happen again
And my smile continues to shine
Because You are always my resting spot
Day after day, my strength renews in You

The Great Unknown

The great unknown
What lies beyond the night
Time in the streets of tomorrow
Will darkness fade
Or be a growing shadow across the face of the earth
The great unknown
A small spark in the midst of blackness
Twinkling past every line in oblivion
Do not fear the star in the darkness
Dark surrounds the steps taken
But the future is not so dim
The great unknown
Help me, Jesus, my Savior
My light in the dark
Your word is my security blanket during the coldest night
Your face I dream when the enemy dances around me
The great unknown
The future is in Your hands
Lives will be touched by Your light in the darkest hour
The great unknown
Marvelous in Your sight
Fear will not hold me back
Because You are Christ, everything I desire
Make Your vessel grow deeper into Your sky
The great unknown
My desires, my heart, fill me with Your presence
Am I a light in the future
Your great unknown

Forever Worship

I'm going to forever worship You
Shout it out at the top of my lungs
Sing it until I'm blue in the face
To forever worship You ...
Makes me whole
When there feels like a hole ...
I worship You
When there is a rip in my soul ...
I worship You
When there is a river flowing down my cheeks ...
I worship You
You have made the strife worth my tears
You have made the journey worth my time
I worship You
When the world is crashing ...
I worship You
When the enemy laughs and dances around me ...
I worship You
Your suffering has hit me hard
I worship You
The trials in my life are a pinch in reality
Nothing is held against me
I worship You
Lord Jesus, I love You
Your whole mind
I worship You

You make me complete
These tears fall hard for You
My world is hard, but because there is You …
It is worthwhile
You make it pleasant
The struggles bring me closer to You
I worship You
As people leave my life …
I will always worship You
There is never a doubt inside me
I will shout my worships
Across the earth, everywhere
There is nothing that can silence me
Jesus, I am worshipping You
Through life and eternity …
I am on my knees

Praise to You Always

Thank You, Jesus!
My mind is too fast for my hand
You utter the most fantastic words
in my life to only give You praise!
I am so thankful I have the privilege to be a part of that
To see Your glory surround me is
changing my life to be as You are
Lord …
I pray for my eyes to always see Your glory
Please allow my heart to remain beside itself
To be always in Your grace
Your glory is all I wish to live for
Tonight and every time I breathe
Let it be only for Your glory, Lord
I love You so much
I long to see Your glory
Mesmerize me, my Lord
So I may always abound in Your grace
Praise to You always
And for the glory of You, my God
I *am* Yours

Bow Down

The wind sweeps across my face
I turn to see
I see brilliant light
Silence dances around me
My eyes stuck on what I see
The gentle wind plays with my hair
My heartbeat echoes through the earth
The most brilliant light I will ever see
Crowding my vision
Heart beating
Breeze blowing
Breath flowing
Oh wow! What a sight!
Your beauty weakens my knees
On my knees You still hold my sight
My ears only hear the sound of a beating heart
The beauty of the brilliance
My hands grasp the greenest grass in front of me
The beat of the heart sounding as thunder
My forehead touches the soft, cool grass
The heartbeat in the silence
The beauty of You brings me to my face
Bowed down in Your presence
Your hand reaches to my head
I feel the love pour over me as You touch me
On my face in the heartbeat of Your love

With one touch, You change my life
The heartbeat still echoes in my ear
The wind still tangles my hair
Grass still clenched between my fingers
Lord, my breath is for You
You say to me in the softest voice …
"You are *Mine,* I will never leave you, because *I* love you"
Heart beating

(Endnotes)

1   John 19:30 NKJV
2   John 19:30 NKJV
3   Luke 23:34 NKJV
4   John 3:16 NKJV